To: Yinya Huang 黃胤雅

From: Carla Moore

Promises and Blessings

© 2005 DaySpring® Cards, Inc.
Siloam Springs, Arkansas

Design by Garborg Design Works

Scripture quotations marked NIV are taken from the Holy Bible, New International Version®. Copyright © 1973, 1978, 1984 by International Bible Society. Used by permission of Zondervan Publishing House.

Scripture quotations marked MSG are taken from The Message. Copyright © 1993, 1994, 1995, 1996. Used by permission of NavPress Publishing Group.

Scripture quotations marked TLB are taken from the The Living Bible © 1971. Used by permission of Tyndale House Publishers, Inc., Wheaton, Illinois 60189. All rights reserved.

ISBN 1-59449-397-9
Printed In China

You who serve God, praise God!
Just to speak his name is praise!
Just to remember God is a blessing now
and tomorrow and always.
From east to west, from dawn to dusk,
keep lifting all your praises to God!

PSALM 113:1-3 MSG

January 1

Remember the former things, those of long ago;
I am God, and there is no other;
I am God, and there is none like me.
I make known the end from the beginning,
from ancient times, what is still to come.
I say: My purpose will stand,
and I will do all that I please.

ISAIAH 46:9–10 NIV

December 31

So I tell you, whatever
you ask for in prayer,
believe that you have received it,
and it will be yours.

MARK 11:24 NRSV

January 2

$\mathcal{L}$o, the star, which they saw in the east, went before them, till it came and stood over where the young child was. And when they were come into the house, they saw the young child with Mary his mother, and fell down, and worshipped him.

MATTHEW 2:9,11 KJV

December 30

*T*hose who hope in the
Lord will renew their strength.
They will soar on wings like eagles;
they will run and not grow weary,
they will walk and not be faint.

ISAIAH 40:31 NIV

January 3

*T*hanks be unto God
for his unspeakable gift.

2 CORINTHIANS 9:15 KJV

December 29

The joy of the Lord
is your strength.

NEHEMIAH 8:10 TLB

January 4

$\mathcal{A}$t once the angel was joined by a huge angelic choir singing God's praises: "Glory to God in the heavenly heights, Peace to all men and women on earth who please him."

LUKE 2:13-14 MSG

December 28

$\mathcal{B}$e still, and know that I am God;
I will be exalted among the nations,
I will be exalted in the earth.

January 5

The dayspring from on high hath visited us, to give light to them that sit in darkness and in the shadow of death, to guide our feet into the way of peace.

LUKE 1:78-79 KJV

December 27

If I speak with the tongues of men and of angels, but do not have love, I have become a noisy gong or a clanging cymbal. And if I have the gift of prophecy, and know all mysteries and all knowledge; and if I have all faith, so as to remove mountains, but do not have love, I am nothing.

1 Corinthians 13:1–2 nasb

January 6

l close my letter with these last words: Be Happy. Grow in Christ. Pay attention to what I have said. Live in harmony and peace. And may the God of love and peace be with you.

2 CORINTHIANS 13:11 TLB

December 26

The Lord is my shepherd, I shall not want. He makes me lie down in green pastures; he leads me beside still waters; he restores my soul. He leads me in right paths for his name's sake. Even though I walk through the darkest valley, I fear no evil; for you are with me; your rod and your staff—they comfort me.

PSALM 23:1-4 NRSV

January 7

For to us a child is born, to us a son is given, and the government will be on his shoulders. And he will be called Wonderful Counselor, Mighty God, Everlasting Father, Prince of Peace.

ISAIAH 9:6 NIV

December 25

$\mathcal{G}$od's peace...is far more wonderful than the human mind can understand. His peace will keep your thoughts and your hearts quiet and at rest as you trust in Christ Jesus.

PHILIPPIANS 4:7 TLB

January 8

$\mathcal{B}$ehold, a virgin shall be with child, and shall bring forth a son, and they shall call his name Emmanuel...God with us.

MATTHEW 1:23 KJV

December 24

Pray without ceasing.

1 THESSALONIANS 5:17 KJV

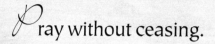

January 9

*B*ut when the time had fully come,
God sent his Son, born of a woman,
born under law, to redeem those under law,
that we might receive the full rights of sons.

GALATIANS 4:4–5 NIV

December 23

I will show kindness to a thousand generations of those who love me and keep my commandments.

DEUTERONOMY 5:10 TLB

January 10

*A*nd the Word was made flesh, and dwelt among us, (and we beheld his glory, the glory as of the only begotten of the Father,) full of grace and truth.

JOHN 1:14 KJV

December 22

Show me your ways, O Lord, teach me your paths; guide me in your truth and teach me, for you are God my Savior, and my hope is in you all day long. Remember, O Lord, your great mercy and love, for they are from of old.

PSALM 25:4-6 NIV

January 11

*A*gain Jesus spoke to them, saying,
"I am the light of the world.
Whoever follows me
will never walk in darkness
but will have the light of life."

JOHN 8:12 NRSV

December 21

$\mathcal{Y}$our heavenly Father knows your
needs. He will always give you all
you need from day to day.

LUKE 12:30-31 TLB

January 12

*M*ercy, peace and love
be yours in abundance.

JUDE 1:2 NIV

December 20

$\mathcal{S}$urprise us with love at daybreak; then we'll skip and dance all the day long.... Let your servants see what you're best at—the ways you rule and bless your children. And let the loveliness of our Lord, our God, rest on us, confirming the work that we do. Oh, yes. Affirm the work that we do!

PSALM 90:14,16–17 MSG

January 13

*F*or we are God's workmanship, created in Christ Jesus to do good works, which God prepared in advance for us to do.

EPHESIANS 2:10 NIV

December 19

Do not let this Book of the Law depart from your mouth; meditate on it day and night, so that you may be careful to do everything written in it. Then you will be prosperous and successful.

JOSHUA 1:8 NIV

January 14

I love them that love me; and those that seek me early shall find me.

PROVERBS 8:17 KJV

December 18

*N*o wonder we are happy in the Lord!
For we are trusting him. We trust
his holy name. Yes, Lord, let your
constant love surround us,
for our hopes are in you alone.

PSALM 33:21-22 TLB

January 15

$\mathcal{N}$ow we can come fearlessly
right into God's presence,
assured of his glad welcome when
we come with Christ and trust in him.

EPHESIANS 3:12 TLB

$\mathcal{December}$ 17

I say to myself, "The Lord is my portion; therefore I will wait for him." The Lord is good to those whose hope is in him, to the one who seeks him; it is good to wait quietly for the salvation of the Lord.

LAMENTATIONS 3:24–26 NIV

January 16

*T*hy word is a lamp unto my feet,
and a light unto my path.

Psalm 119:105 KJV

December 16

I am with you, and will protect you wherever you go.

GENESIS 28:15 TLB

January 17

$\mathcal{E}$ach one should use whatever gift he has received to serve others, faithfully administering God's grace in its various forms.

1 PETER 4:10 NIV

$\mathcal{D}$ecember 15

The promise of "arrival" and "rest" is still there for God's people. God himself is at rest. And at the end of the journey we'll surely rest with God. So let's keep at it and eventually arrive at the place of rest, not drop out through some sort of disobedience.

HEBREWS 4:9-11 MSG

January 18

*F*or if you give, you will get! Your gift will return to you in full and overflowing measure, pressed down, shaken together to make room for more, and running over. Whatever measure you use to give—large or small—will be used to measure what is given back to you.

LUKE 6:38 TLB

December 14

*H*onor and majesty
are before him;
strength and beauty
are in his sanctuary.

PSALM 96:6 NRSV

January 19

Send forth your light and your truth, let them guide me; let them bring me to your holy mountain, to the place where you dwell. Then will I go to the altar of God, to God, my joy and my delight.

PSALM 43:3-4 NIV

December 13

Therefore, since we have been justified through faith, we have peace with God through our Lord Jesus Christ, through whom we have gained access by faith into this grace in which we now stand. And we rejoice in the hope of the glory of God.

ROMANS 5:1-2 NIV

January 20

It is more blessed
to give than to receive.

Acts 20:35 kjv

December 12

$\mathcal{M}$y heart took
delight in all my work,
and this was the reward
for all my labor.

ECCLESIASTES 2:10 NIV

January 21

*T*hen the Lord God will wipe away
the tears from all faces, and the
disgrace of his people he will
take away from all the earth,
for the Lord has spoken.

December 11

$\mathcal{L}$ike apples of gold in settings of silver
Is a word spoken in right circumstances.
Like an earring of gold and
an ornament of fine gold
Is a wise reprover to a listening ear.

PROVERBS 25:11-12 NASB

January 22

$\mathcal{M}$y frame was not hidden from you when I was made in the secret place. When I was woven together in the depths of the earth, your eyes saw my unformed body. All the days ordained for me were written in your book before one of them came to be.

PSALM 139:15–16 NIV

December 10

I am the Lord your God,
who brought you out of Egypt,
out of the land of slavery.
You shall have no other
gods before me.

EXODUS 20:2-3 NIV

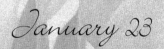

January 23

I thank my God always concerning you, for the grace of God which was given you in Christ Jesus, that in everything you were enriched in Him, in all speech and all knowledge, even as the testimony concerning Christ was confirmed in you, so that you are not lacking in any gift, awaiting eagerly the revelation of your Lord Jesus Christ.

1 CORINTHIANS 1:4-7 NASB

December 9

*L*ove knows no limit
to its endurance,
no end to its trust,
no fading of its hope;
it can outlast anything.
Love never fails.

1 CORINTHIANS 13:7-8 PHILLIPS

January 24

$\mathcal{G}$od is one and there is no other. And loving him with all passion and intelligence and energy, and loving others as well as you love yourself. Why, that's better than all offerings and sacrifices put together!

MARK 12:32-33 MSG

December 8

$\mathcal{N}$ow God, don't hold out on me,
don't hold back your passion.
Your love and truth are all
that keeps me together.

PSALM 40:11 MSG

January 25

*F*or you know the grace of our
Lord Jesus Christ, that though
he was rich, yet for your sakes
he became poor, so that
you through his poverty
might become rich.

2 CORINTHIANS 8:9 NIV

December 7

With the Lord a day is like a thousand years, and a thousand years are like a day. The Lord is not slow in keeping his promise, as some understand slowness. He is patient with you, not wanting anyone to perish, but everyone to come to repetance.

2 PETER 3:8-9 NIV

January 26

$\mathcal{O}$, God, in mercy bless us; let your face beam with joy as you look down at us.

PSALM 67:1 TLB

December 6

$\mathcal{A}$nd straightway the father
of the child cried out, and said
with tears, Lord, I believe;
help thou mine unbelief.

MARK 9:24 KJV

January 27

*W*orship the Lord your God and only the Lord your God. Serve Him with absolute single-heartedness.

LUKE 4:8 MSG

December 5

$\mathcal{M}$ay the Lord
continually bless you
with heaven's blessings
as well as with human joys.

PSALM 128:5 TLB

January 28

$\mathcal{M}$ay God who gives patience, steadiness, and encouragement help you to live in complete harmony with each other.

ROMANS 15:5 TLB

December 4

*F*orget the former things;
do not dwell on the past.
See, I am doing a new thing!
Now it springs up; do you
not perceive it?
I am making a way in the desert
and streams in the wasteland.

ISAIAH 43:18–19 NIV

January 29

*W*here can I go from your Spirit? Where can I flee from your presence? If I go up to the heavens, you are there; if I make my bed in the depths, you are there. If I rise on the wings of the dawn, if I settle on the far side of the sea, even there your hand will guide me, your right hand will hold me fast.

PSALM 139:7-10 NIV

December 3

O sing to the Lord a new song;
sing to the Lord, all the earth.
Sing to the Lord, bless his name;
tell of his salvation from day to day.
Declare his glory among the nations, his
marvelous works among all the peoples.

PSALM 96:1-3 NRSV

January 30

$\mathcal{A}$sk, and it shall be given to you;
seek, and you shall find; knock,
and it shall be opened to you.
For everyone who asks,
receives; and he who seeks,
finds; and to him who knocks,
it shall be opened.

LUKE 11:9-10 NASB

$\mathcal{A}$ville 2

*W*hat a wonderful God we have—he is the Father of our Lord Jesus Christ, the source of every mercy, and the one who so wonderfully comforts and strengthens us in our hardships and trials.

2 CORINTHIANS 1:3-4 TLB

January 31

The Lord says, "I will make my people strong with power from me!... Wherever they go, they will be under my personal care."

ZECHARIAH 10:12 TLB

December 1

The Lord is in his holy temple;
the Lord is on his heavenly throne.
He observes the sons of men;
his eyes examine them....
For the Lord is righteous,
he loves justice; upright
men will see his face.

PSALM 11:4,7 NIV

February 1

*P*raise ye the Lord. Praise God in his sanctuary: praise him in the firmament of his power. Praise him for his mighty acts: praise him according to his excellent greatness.... Let every thing that hath breath praise the Lord. Praise ye the Lord.

PSALM 150:1-2,6 KJV

November 30

$\mathcal{M}$ay God, who puts all things together, makes all things whole... Who led Jesus, our Great Shepherd, up and alive from the dead, Now put you together, provide you with everything you need to please him...by means of the sacrifice of Jesus, the Messiah. All glory to Jesus forever and always!

HEBREWS 13:20–21 MSG

February 2

$\mathcal{B}$ut he said to me, "My grace is sufficient for you, for my power is made perfect in weakness." Therefore I will boast all the more gladly about my weaknesses, so that Christ's power may rest on me.

2 CORINTHIANS 12:9 NIV

November 29

*F*or though we have never yet seen God,
when we love each other God lives in us
and his love within us grows ever stronger.

1 JOHN 4:12 TLB

February 3

$\mathscr{Y}$ou're blessed when you're content with just who you are—no more, no less. That's the moment you find yourselves proud owners of everything that can't be bought. You're blessed when you've worked up a good appetite for God. He's food and drink in the best meal you'll ever eat.

MATTHEW 5:5-6 MSG

November 28

$\mathcal{T}$wo are better than one; because they have a good reward for their labour. For if they fall, the one will lift up his fellow: but woe to him that is alone when he falleth; for he hath not another to help him up.

ECCLESIASTES 4:9-10 KJV

February 4

Search me, O God, and know my heart;
test me and know my anxious thoughts.
See if there is any offensive way in me,
and lead me in the way everlasting.

PSALM 139:23-24 NIV

November 27

The Lord is my light and my salvation—
whom shall I fear?
The Lord is the stronghold of my life—
of whom shall I be afraid?

PSALM 27:1 NIV

February 5

Give thanks to the Lord, for he is good.
His love endures forever. Give thanks to
the God of gods. His love endures forever.
Give thanks to the Lord of lords:
His love endures forever. To him
who alone does great wonders,
His love endures forever.

PSALM 136:1-4 NIV

November 26

I have loved you with
an everlasting love;
therefore I have continued
my faithfulness to you.

JEREMIAH 31:3 NRSV

February 6

We always thank God for all of you,
mentioning you in our prayers.

1 THESSALONIANS 1:2 NIV

November 25

For my thoughts are not your thoughts,
neither are your ways my ways,
saith the Lord. For as the heavens are
higher than the earth, so are my ways
higher than your ways, and my
thoughts than your thoughts.

Isaiah 55:8–9 KJV

February 7

*C*ast thy burden upon the Lord,
and he shall sustain thee:
he shall never suffer the
righteous to be moved.

PSALM 55:22 KJV

November 24

May the God of hope fill you
with all joy and peace as you
trust in him, so that you
may overflow with hope
by the power of the Holy Spirit.

ROMANS 15:13 NIV

February 8

*A*lways be joyful.
Always keep on praying.
No matter what happens,
always be thankful, for
this is God's will for you
who belong to Christ Jesus.

1 THESSALONIANS 5:16–18 TLB

November 23

*H*e is good to everyone, and his compassion is intertwined with everything he does.

PSALM 145:9 TLB

February 9

O Lord, you are my God;
I will exalt you and praise your
name, for in perfect faithfulness
you have done marvelous things,
things planned long ago.

ISAIAH 25:1 NIV

November 22

*W*ithout faith it is impossible to please God, because anyone who comes to him must believe that he exists and that he rewards those who earnestly seek him.

HEBREWS 11:6 NIV

February 10

There is no room in love for fear.
Well-formed love banishes fear.
Since fear is crippling,
a fearful life—fear of death,
fear of judgment—is one
not yet fully formed in love.

1 JOHN 4:18 MSG

November 21

The Lord will keep you from all harm—
he will watch over your life; the Lord
will watch over your coming and
going both now and forevermore.

PSALM 121:7-8 NIV

February 11

These things I have spoken unto you, that in me ye might have peace. In the world ye shall have tribulation: but be of good cheer; I have overcome the world.

JOHN 16:33 KJV

November 20

With respect to the promise of God, he did not waver in unbelief, but grew strong in faith, giving glory to God, and being fully assured that what He had promised, He was able also to perform.

ROMANS 4:20-21 NASB

February 12

The Sovereign Lord is my strength;
he makes my feet like the feet of a deer,
he enables me to go on the heights.

HABAKKUK 3:19 NIV

November 19

Then I lay down and slept in peace and woke up safely, for the Lord was watching over me. And now, although ten thousand enemies surround me on every side, I am not afraid.

PSALM 3:5-6 TLB

February 13

I will give you one heart and a new spirit;
I will take from you your hearts of stone and
give you tender hearts of love for your God.

EZEKIEL 11:19 TLB

November 18

*A*nd now these three remain:
faith, hope and love.
But the greatest of these is love.

1 CORINTHIANS 13:13 NIV

February 14

$\mathcal{W}$hat a wildly wonderful world, God! You made it all, with Wisdom at your side, made earth overflow with your wonderful creations.... All the creatures look expectantly to you.... The glory of God—let it last forever! Let God enjoy his creation!

PSALM 104:24,27,31 MSG

November 17

May the Lord make your love increase and
overflow for each other and for everyone else,
just as ours does for you. May he strengthen
your hearts so that you will be blameless
and holy in the presence of our God
and Father when our Lord Jesus
comes with all his holy ones.

1 THESSALONIANS 3:12–13 NIV

February 15

You also were included in Christ when you heard the word of truth, the gospel of your salvation. Having believed, you were marked in him with a seal, the promised Holy Spirit.

EPHESIANS 1:13 NIV

November 16

Our help is in the name of the Lord,
who made heaven and earth.

PSALM 124:8 KJV

February 16

$\mathcal{L}$isten, I will tell you a mystery! We will not all die, but we will all be changed, in a moment, in the twinkling of an eye, at the last trumpet. For the trumpet will sound, and the dead will be raised imperishable, and we will be changed.

1 CORINTHIANS 15:51–52 NRSV

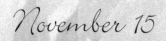

November 15

Commit your work
to the Lord,
and your plans
will be established.

PROVERBS 16:3 NRSV

February 17

*B*ut if...you seek the Lord your God,
you will find him if you look for him
with all your heart and with all your soul.

DEUTERONOMY 4:29 NIV

November 14

In him we have redemption through his blood, the forgiveness of sins, in accordance with the riches of God's grace that he lavished on us with all wisdom and understanding.

EPHESIANS 1:7-8 NIV

February 18

It's who you are and the way you live that count before God. Your worship must engage your spirit in the pursuit of truth. That's the kind of people the Father is out looking for: those who are simply and honestly themselves before him in their worship. God is sheer being itself—Spirit. Those who worship him must do it out of their very being, their spirits, their true selves, in adoration.

JOHN 4:23-24 MSG

November 13

May God himself, the God of peace,
sanctify you through and through.
May your whole spirit, soul and
body be kept blameless at the
coming of our Lord Jesus Christ.
The one who calls you is
faithful and he will do it.

1 Thessalonians 5:23-24 niv

February 19

*F*or our light affliction, which is for a moment, worketh for us a far more exceeding and eternal weight of glory.

2 CORINTHIANS 4:17 KJV

November 12

*I*sn't everything you have and everything you are sheer gifts from God?... You already have all you need.

1 CORINTHIANS 4:7-8 MSG

February 20

I appeal to you therefore, brothers and sisters, by the mercies of God, to present your bodies as a living sacrifice, holy and acceptable to God, which is your spiritual worship. Do not be conformed to this world, but be transformed by the renewing of your minds, so that you may discern what is the will of God— what is good and acceptable and perfect.

ROMANS 12:1–2 NRSV

November 11

$\mathcal{O}$ne thing have I desired of the Lord, that will I seek after; that I may dwell in the house of the Lord all the days of my life, to behold the beauty of the Lord, and to inquire in his temple. For in the time of trouble he shall hide me in his pavilion: in the secret of his tabernacle shall he hide me; he shall set me up upon a rock.

PSALM 27:4–5 NIV

February 21

For as the rain and the snow
come down from heaven,
And do not return there without watering the earth....
So shall My word be which
goes forth from My mouth;
It shall not return to Me empty,
Without accomplishing what I desire.

ISAIAH 55:10–11 NASB

November 10

$\mathcal{J}$esus said to her, "Everyone who drinks of this water will be thirsty again, but those who drink of the water that I will give them will never be thirsty. The water that I will give will become in them a spring of water gushing up to eternal life."

JOHN 4:13–14 NRSV

February 22

$\mathcal{W}$ho is a God like you, who pardons sin...? You do not stay angry forever but delight to show mercy. You will again have compassion on us.

MICAH 7:18–19 NIV

November 9

I urge you to live a life worthy of
the calling you have received.
Be completely humble and gentle;
be patient, bearing with
one another in love.

EPHESIANS 4:1–2 NIV

February 23

Every morning tell him, "Thank you for your kindness," and every evening rejoice in all his faithfulness.

PSALM 92:2 TLB

November 8

All thy works shall praise thee, O Lord; and thy saints shall bless thee. They shall speak of the glory of thy kingdom, and talk of thy power; To make known to the sons of men his mighty acts, and the glorious majesty of his kingdom. Thy kingdom is an everlasting kingdom, and thy dominion endureth throughout all generations.

PSALM 145:10-13 KJV

February 24

$\mathcal{P}$raise be to the God and Father of our Lord Jesus Christ, who has blessed us in the heavenly realms with every spiritual blessing in Christ. For he chose us in him before the creation of the world to be holy and blameless in his sight.

EPHESIANS 1:3-4 NIV

November 7

*P*ure gold put in the fire comes out of it proved pure; genuine faith put through this suffering comes out proved genuine. When Jesus wraps this all up, it's your faith, not your gold, that God will have on display as evidence of his victory.

1 PETER 1:7 MSG

February 25

The Lord does not see as mortals see;
they look on the outward appearance,
but the Lord looks on the heart.

1 SAMUEL 16:7 NRSV

November 6

Don't worry about anything; instead, pray about everything; tell God your needs, and don't forget to thank him for his answers.

PHILIPPIANS 4:6 TLB

February 26

*F*or you created my inmost being; you
knit me together in my mother's womb.
I praise you because I am fearfully
and wonderfully made;
your works are wonderful,
I know that full well.

PSALM 139:13–14 NIV

November 5

In love he predestined us to be adopted
as his sons through Jesus Christ, in
accordance with his pleasure and will—
to the praise of his glorious grace, which
he has freely given us in the One he loves.

EPHESIANS 1:4-6 NIV

February 27

I am the Vine, you are the branches. When you're joined with me and I with you, the relation intimate and organic, the harvest is sure to be abundant.

JOHN 15:5 MSG

November 4

The Lord is gracious,
and full of compassion;
slow to anger,
and of great mercy.

PSALM 145:8 KJV

February 28

*B*ut whatever was to my profit I now consider loss for the sake of Christ. What is more, I consider everything a loss compared to the surpassing greatness of knowing Christ Jesus my Lord.... That I may gain Christ and be found in him, not having a righteousness of my own that comes from the law, but that which is through faith in Christ.

PHILIPPIANS 3:7–9 NIV

November 3

$\mathcal{W}$e also rejoice in our sufferings, because we know that suffering produces perseverance; perseverance, character; and character, hope. And hope does not disappoint us, because God has poured out his love into our hearts by the Holy Spirit, whom he has given us.

ROMANS 5:3-5 NIV

February 29

Create in me a clean heart, O God; and renew a right spirit within me. Cast me not away from thy presence; and take not thy holy spirit from me. Restore unto me the joy of thy salvation; and uphold me with thy free spirit.

PSALM 51:10–12 KJV

November 2

God made my life complete when
I placed all the pieces before him.
When I got my act together,
he gave me a fresh start....
God rewrote the text of my life
when I opened the book
of my heart to his eyes.

PSALM 18:20,24 MSG

March 1

O Lord, you are our Father. We are
the clay and you are the Potter. We
are all formed by your hand.

ISAIAH 64:8 TLB

November 1

But each of us was given grace
according to the measure
of Christ's gift.

EPHESIANS 4:7 NRSV

March 2

I will pour out my Spirit on all people. Your sons and daughters will prophesy, your old men will dream dreams, your young men will see visions. Even on my servants, both men and women, I will pour out my Spirit in those days. I will show wonders in the heavens and on the earth.

JOEL 2:28-30 NIV

October 31

I wait for the Lord, my soul waits, and in his word I put my hope. My soul waits for the Lord more than watchmen wait for the morning, more than watchmen wait for the morning.

PSALM 130:5-6 NIV

March 3

Real wisdom, God's wisdom, begins with a holy life and is characterized by getting along with others. It is gentle and reasonable, overflowing with mercy and blessings, not hot one day and cold the next, not two-faced. You can develop a healthy, robust community that lives right with God and enjoy its results only if you do the hard work of getting along with each other, treating each other with dignity and honor.

JAMES 3:17-18 MSG

October 30

We throw open our doors to God and discover at the same moment that he has already thrown open his door to us. We find ourselves standing where we always hoped we might stand out in the wide open spaces of God's grace and glory, standing tall and shouting our praise.

Romans 5:2 MSG

March 4

I pray also that the eyes of your heart may be enlightened in order that you may know the hope to which he has called you, the riches of his glorious inheritance in the saints, and his incomparably great power for us who believe.

EPHESIANS 1:18–19 NIV

October 29

*A*nd he said, Go forth, and stand upon the mount before the Lord. And, behold, the Lord passed by, and a great and strong wind rent the mountains...but the Lord was not in the wind: and after the wind an earthquake; but the Lord was not in the earthquake: And after the earthquake a fire; but the Lord was not in the fire: and after the fire a still small voice. And it was so.

1 KINGS 19:11-13 KJV

March 5

*H*umble yourselves therefore
under the mighty hand of God,
that he may exalt you in due time:
Casting all your care upon him;
for he careth for you.

1 Peter 5:6-7 KJV

October 28

l will refresh the weary
and satisfy the faint.

JEREMIAH 31:25 NIV

March 6

For the Lord takes delight in his people;
he crowns the humble with salvation.
Let the saints rejoice in this honor
and sing for joy.

PSALM 149:4-5 NIV

October 27

*R*emember that at that time you were separate from Christ...without hope and without God in the world. But now in Christ Jesus you who once were far away have been brought near through the blood of Christ.

EPHESIANS 2:12-13 NIV

March 7

Search high and low, scan skies and land,
you'll find nothing and no one quite like God.
The holy angels are in awe before him;
He looms immense and august over
everyone around him. God...who is
like you, powerful and faithful
from every angle?

PSALM 89:6-8 MSG

October 26

*A*h Lord God! behold, thou hast made the heaven and the earth by thy great power and stretched out arm, and there is nothing too hard for thee.

JEREMIAH 32:17 KJV

March 8

$\mathcal{L}$ove is patient, love is kind. It does not envy, it does not boast, it is not proud. It is not rude, it is not self-seeking, it is not easily angered, it keeps no record of wrongs. Love does not delight in evil but rejoices with the truth.

1 CORINTHIANS 13:4–5 NIV

October 25

*A*re not five sparrows sold for two pennies? Yet not one of them is forgotten in God's sight. But even the hairs of your head are all counted. Do not be afraid; you are of more value than many sparrows.

LUKE 12:6–7 NRSV

March 9

*I*n returning and rest shall ye be saved;
in quietness and in confidence
shall be your strength.

ISAIAH 30:15 KJV

October 24

*H*ave mercy on me, O God, according to your unfailing love; according to your great compassion blot out my transgressions.... Wash me, and I will be whiter than snow.

PSALM 51:1,7 NIV

March 10

$\mathcal{L}$et us draw near to God with a sincere heart in full assurance of faith.... Let us hold unswervingly to the hope we profess, for he who promised is faithful. And let us consider how we may spur one another on toward love and good deeds. Let us not give up meeting together...but let us encourage one another—and all the more as you see the Day approaching.

HEBREWS 10:22-25 NIV

A A A A A

October 23

*F*inally, my brethren,
be strong in the Lord, and
in the power of his might.

EPHESIANS 6:10 KJV

March 11

I will love thee, O Lord, my strength. The Lord is my rock, and my fortress, and my deliverer; my God, my strength, in whom I will trust; my buckler, and the horn of my salvation, and my high tower. I will call upon the Lord, who is worthy to be praised: so shall I be saved from mine enemies.

PSALM 18:1-3 NIV

October 22

*C*ontinue your love to those who
know you, your righteousness
to the upright in heart.

PSALM 36:10 NIV

March 12

*G*od demonstrates His love toward us,
in that, while we were yet sinners,
Christ died for us.

Romans 5:8 nrsv

October 21

$\mathcal{G}$od is able to make all grace abound to you, so that in all things at all times, having all that you need, you will abound in every good work.

2 CORINTHIANS 9:8 NIV

March 13

*T*o every thing there is a season, and a
time to every purpose under the heaven.

ECCLESIASTES 3:1 KJV

October 20

*F*or the word of God is living and active. Sharper than any double-edged sword, it penetrates even to dividing soul and spirit, joints and marrow; it judges the thoughts and attitudes of the heart.

HEBREWS 4:12 NIV

March 14

*H*e said to his disciples, "Therefore I tell you, do not worry about your life, what you will eat, or about your body, what you will wear. For life is more than food, and the body more than clothing. Consider the ravens: they neither sow nor reap, they have neither storehouse nor barn, and yet God feeds them. Of how much more value are you than the birds!"

LUKE 12:22–24 NRSV

October 19

l delight to do Thy will, O my God;
Thy Law is within my heart.

PSALM 40:8 NASB

March 15

For I will pour water on the thirsty land,
and streams on the dry ground;
I will pour out my Spirit on your offspring,
and my blessing on your descendants.

ISAIAH 44:3 NIV

October 18

*W*ho shall separate us from the love of Christ? Shall trouble or hardship or persecution or famine or nakedness or sword? No, in all these things we are more than conquerors through him who loved us.

ROMANS 8:35–37 NIV

March 16

How ow precious to me are your thoughts,
O God! How vast is the sum of them!
Were I to count them, they would
outnumber the grains of sand.

PSALM 139:17–18 NIV

October 17

*H*e raised [Christ] from the dead and seated him at his right hand in the heavenly realms, far above all rule and authority, power and dominion, and every title that can be given, not only in the present age but also in the one to come.

EPHESIANS 1:20-21 NIV

March 17

$\mathcal{A}$t the time, discipline isn't much fun. It always feels like it's going against the grain. Later, of course, it pays off handsomely, for it's the well-trained who find themselves mature in their relationship with God.

HEBREWS 12:11 MSG

October 16

The world of the generous gets larger and larger.... The one who blesses others is abundantly blessed; those who help others are helped.

PROVERBS 11:24-25 MSG

March 18

I sought the Lord, and he answered me;
he delivered me from all my fears.
Those who look to him are radiant;
their faces are never covered with shame.

PSALM 34:4-5 NIV

October 15

*B*ut all who humble themselves before the Lord shall be given every blessing, and shall have wonderful peace.

PSALM 37:11 TLB

March 19

$\mathscr{T}$he human mind plans the way,
but the Lord directs the steps.

PROVERBS 16:9 NRSV

October 14

All Scripture is inspired by God and
profitable for teaching, for reproof,
for correction, for training in righteousness.

2 TIMOTHY 3:16 NASB

March 20

$\mathcal{W}$ait on the Lord: be of good courage,
and he shall strengthen thine heart:
wait, I say, on the Lord.

PSALM 27:14 KJV

October 13

Delight yourself in the Lord and he will
give you the desires of your heart.
Commit your way to the Lord;
trust in him and he will do this:
He will make your righteousness shine
like the dawn, the justice of your cause
like the noonday sun.

PSALM 37:4-6 NIV

March 21

l want to know Christ and the power of his resurrection and the fellowship of sharing in his sufferings, becoming like him in his death, and so, somehow, to attain to the resurrection from the dead. Not that I have already obtained all this, or have already been made perfect, but I press on to take hold of that for which Christ Jesus took hold of me.

PHILIPPIANS 3:10-12 NIV

October 12

I truly delight in God's commands, but it's pretty obvious that not all of me joins in that delight. Parts of me covertly rebel, and just when I least expect it, they take charge. I've tried everything and nothing helps. I'm at the end of my rope. Is there no one who can do anything for me? Isn't that the real question? The answer, thank God, is that Jesus Christ can and does.

ROMANS 7:22-25 MSG

March 22

$\mathcal{G}$od is sheer mercy and grace; not easily angered, he's rich in love.... He doesn't treat us as our sins deserve, nor pay us back in full for our wrongs. As high as heaven is over the earth, so strong is his love to those who fear him. And as far as sunrise is from sunset, he has separated us from our sins.

PSALM 103:8, 10-12 MSG

October 11

*A*bove all else, guard your affections. For they influence everything else in your life.

PROVERBS 4:23 TLB

March 23

*N*ow faith is being sure of what we hope for and certain of what we do not see.... By faith Abel offered God a better sacrifice than Cain did. By faith he was commended as a righteous man, when God spoke well of his offerings. And by faith he still speaks, even though he is dead.

HEBREWS 11:1,4 NIV

October 10

$\mathcal{F}$or you were going astray like sheep,
but now you have returned to the
shepherd and guardian of your souls.

1 PETER 2:25 NRSV

March 24

*Y*ou know with all your heart and soul that not one of all the good promises the Lord your God gave you has failed. Every promise has been fulfilled; not one has failed.

JOSHUA 23:14 NIV

October 9

*O*pen your mouth and taste, open your eyes and see how good God is. Blessed are you who run to him. Worship God if you want the best; worship opens doors to all his goodness.

PSALM 34:8-9 MSG

March 25

Our Father which art in heaven,
Hallowed be thy name. Thy kingdom come. Thy will
be done in earth, as it is in heaven. Give us this day our
daily bread. And forgive us our debts, as we forgive our
debtors. And lead us not into temptation, but deliver us
from evil: For thine is the kingdom, and the power,
and the glory, for ever. Amen.

MATTHEW 6:9-13 KJV

October 8

No eye has seen,
no ear has heard,
no mind has conceived
what God has prepared
for those who love him.

1 CORINTHIANS 2:9 NIV

March 26

I have set the Lord always before me.
Because he is at my right hand, I will not
be shaken. Therefore my heart is glad
and my tongue rejoices; my body
also will rest secure.

PSALM 16:8–9 NIV

October 7

$\mathcal{N}$ot to us, O Lord, not to us, but to your name give glory, for the sake of your steadfast love and your faithfulness.

PSALM 115:1 NRSV

March 27

May our Lord Jesus Christ himself
and God our Father, who loved us
and by his grace gave us eternal
encouragement and good hope,
encourage your hearts and strengthen
you in every good deed and word.

2 THESSALONIANS 2:16–17 NIV

October 6

*W*hen you draw close to God,
God will draw close to you.

JAMES 4:8 TLB

March 28

$\mathcal{M}$any are saying to me, "There is no help for you in God." But you, O Lord, are a shield around me, my glory, and the one who lifts up my head. I cry aloud to the Lord, and he answers me from his holy hill.

PSALM 3:3-4 NRSV

$\mathcal{October}$ 5

$\mathcal{T}$he Lord is my strength and my shield;
my heart trusts in him, and I am helped.

PSALM 28:7 NIV

March 29

Rejoice in the Lord your God, for he has given you the autumn rains in righteousness. He sends you abundant showers, both autumn and spring rains, as before. The threshing floors will be filled with grain; the vats will overflow with new wine and oil.

JOEL 2:23-25 NIV

October 4

$\mathcal{T}$he first thing I want you to do is pray. Pray every way you know how, for everyone you know. Pray especially for rulers and their governments to rule well so we can be quietly about our business of living simply, in humble contemplation. This is the way our Savior God wants us to live.

1 TIMOTHY 2:1-3 MSG

March 30

God's Spirit is right alongside helping us along. If we don't know how or what to pray, it doesn't matter. He does our praying in and for us, making prayer out of our wordless sighs, our aching groans. He knows us far better than we know ourselves...and keeps us present before God. That's why we can be so sure that every detail in our lives of love for God is worked into something good.

ROMANS 8:26-28 MSG

October 3

So be truly glad! There is wonderful joy ahead, even though the going is rough for a while down here.... You love him even though you have never seen him; though not seeing him, you trust him; and even now you are happy with the inexpressible joy that comes from heaven itself.

1 PETER 1:6,8 TLB

March 31

*T*he Lord...is righteous; he
does no wrong. Morning by
morning he dispenses his
justice, and every new
day he does not fail.

ZEPHANIAH 3:5 NIV

October 2

O how abundant is your goodness that you have laid up for those who fear you, and accomplished for those who take refuge in you, in the sight of everyone!

PSALM 31:19 NRSV

April 1

I will lie down and sleep in peace,
for you alone, O Lord, make me
dwell in safety.

PSALM 4:8 NIV

October 1

*W*hat marvelous love the Father has extended to us! Just look at it we're called children of God! That's who we really are.

1 JOHN 3:1 MSG

April 2

$\mathcal{W}$e all live off his generous bounty,
   gift after gift after gift...
this exuberant giving and receiving,
This endless knowing and understanding—
   all this came through Jesus,
the Messiah.

JOHN 1:16-17 MSG

September 30

*Y*our word, O Lord, is eternal; it stands firm in the heavens. Your faithfulness continues through all generations; you established the earth, and it endures. Your laws endure to this day.

PSALM 119:89–91 NIV

April 3

*Y*ou give them drink
from your river of delights.
For with you is the fountain of life;
in your light we see light.

PSALM 36:8-9 NIV

September 29

Whither thou goest, I will go; and where thou lodgest, I will lodge: thy people shall be my people, and thy God my God.

RUTH 1:16 KJV

April 4

He is not far from each one of us. For in him we live and move and have our being.

ACTS 17:27-28 NIV

September 28

$\mathcal{M}$ay you be given more and more
of God's kindness, peace, and love.

JUDE 1:2 TLB

April 5

I will bless the Lord at all times; His praise shall continually be in my mouth.

September 27

I will send down showers in season;
there will be showers of blessing.

EZEKIEL 34:26 NIV

April 6

*H*e shall feed his flock like a shepherd:
he shall gather the lambs with his arm,
and carry them in his bosom, and shall
gently lead those that are with young.

ISAIAH 40:11 KJV

September 26

*F*inally, brothers, whatever is true, whatever is noble, whatever is right, whatever is pure, whatever is lovely, whatever is admirable—if anything is excellent or praiseworthy— think about such things.

PHILIPPIANS 4:8 NIV

April 7

May the Lord, the God of your fathers,
increase you a thousand times and
bless you as he has promised!

DEUTERONOMY 1:11 NIV

September 25

Be kind to one another, tenderhearted,
forgiving one another, as God
in Christ has forgiven you.

EPHESIANS 4:32 NRSV

April 8

You're my place of quiet retreat;
I wait for your Word to renew me...
therefore I lovingly embrace
everything you say.

PSALM 119:114,119 MSG

September 24

$\mathcal{H}$e is like a father to us, tender and sympathetic to those who reverence him. For he knows we are but dust, and that our days are few and brief, like grass, like flowers, blown by the wind and gone forever.

PSALM 103:13–15 TLB

April 9

*F*or the earth shall be filled
with the knowledge of
the glory of the Lord,
as the waters cover the sea.

HABAKKUK 2:14 KJV

September 23

$\mathcal{N}$ow upon the first day of the week, very early in the morning, they came unto the sepulchre.... And they found the stone rolled away from the sepulchre. And they entered in, and found not the body of the Lord Jesus. And...behold, two men stood by them in shining garments: And as they were afraid, and bowed down their faces to the earth, they said unto them, Why seek ye the living among the dead? He is not here, but is risen.

LUKE 24:1-6 KJV

April 10

The Lord is slow to anger and great in power; the Lord will not leave the guilty unpunished. His way is in the whirlwind and the storm, and clouds are the dust of his feet.

NAHUM 1:3 NIV

September 22

$\mathcal{G}$od does not respond to what we do;
we respond to what God does. We've
finally figured it out. Our lives get
in step with God and all others
by letting him set the pace,
not by proudly or anxiously
trying to run the parade.

Romans 3:27-28 msg

April 11

It is you who light my lamp; the Lord,
my God, lights up my darkness.
By you I can crush a troop, and by
my God I can leap over a wall.

PSALM 18:28-29 NRSV

September 21

*A*sk the Lord for rain in the springtime;
it is the Lord who makes the storm clouds.
He gives showers of rain to men,
and plants of the field to everyone.

ZECHARIAH 10:1 NIV

April 12

*N*o test or temptation that comes your way is beyond the course of what others have had to face. All you need to remember is that God will never let you down; he'll never let you be pushed past your limit; he'll always be there to help you come through it.

1 CORINTHIANS 10:13 MSG

September 20

*B*less the Lord, O my soul,

And forget none of His benefits;

Who pardons all your iniquities;

Who heals all your diseases.

Who redeems your life from the pit;

Who crowns you with lovingkindness and compassion;

Who satisfies your years with good things,

So that your youth is renewed like the eagle.

PSALM 103:2-3 NASB

April 13

*B*ut let all who take refuge in you be glad; let them ever sing for joy. Spread your protection over them, that those who love your name may rejoice in you. For surely, O Lord, you bless the righteous; you surround them with your favor as with a shield.

PSALM 5:11-12 NIV

September 19

If my people, which are called by my name, shall humble themselves, and pray, and seek my face, and turn from their wicked ways; then will I hear from heaven, and will forgive their sin, and will heal their land.

2 Chronicles 7:14 KJV

April 14

$\mathcal{L}$ove your enemies. Let them bring out the best in you, not the worst. When someone gives you a hard time, respond with the energies of prayer, for then you are working out of your true selves, your God-created selves. This is what God does. He gives his best—the sun to warm and the rain to nourish—to everyone.

MATTHEW 5:44-45 MSG

September 18

*H*ear my cry, O God; listen to my prayer.
From the ends of the earth I call to you,
I call as my heart grows faint; lead me
to the rock that is higher than I.
For you have been my refuge.

PSALM 61:1-3 NIV

April 15

Come, and let us go up to the mountain of the Lord...and he will teach us of his ways, and we will walk in his paths.

MICAH 4:2 KJV

September 17

$\mathcal{T}$hen I looked, and I heard the voice of many angels...singing with full voice, "Worthy is the Lamb."

REVELATION 5:11-12 NRSV

April 16

*T*he Spirit of the Sovereign Lord is on me, because the Lord has anointed me to preach good news to the poor. He has sent me to bind up the brokenhearted, to proclaim freedom for the captives and release from darkness for the prisoners.

ISAIAH 61:1 NIV

September 16

The Lord bless thee, and keep thee:
the Lord make his face shine upon thee,
and be gracious unto thee: the Lord
lift up his countenance upon thee,
and give thee peace.

NUMBERS 6:24-26 KJV

April 17

*I*n him we were also chosen, having been predestined according to the plan of him who works out everything in conformity with the purpose of his will, in order that we, who were the first to hope in Christ, might be for the praise of his glory.

EPHESIANS 1:11–12 NIV

September 15

$\mathcal{M}$ay the love and favor of the
Lord Jesus Christ rest upon you.

1 CORINTHIANS 16:23 TLB

April 18

My help comes from the Lord, who made heaven and earth. He...will neither slumber nor sleep. The Lord is your keeper; the Lord is your shade at your right hand.

PSALM 121:2,4-5 NRSV

September 14

F or God is sheer beauty,
all-generous in love,
loyal always and ever.

PSALM 100:5 MSG

April 19

Encourage one another daily, as long as it is called Today.... We have come to share in Christ if we hold firmly till the end the confidence we had at first.

HEBREWS 3:13–14 NIV

September 13

The heavens declare the glory of God;
the skies proclaim the work of his hands.
Day after day they pour forth speech;
night after night they display knowledge.

PSALM 19:1-2 NIV

April 20

$\mathcal{F}$or you will go out with joy,
And be led forth with peace;
The mountains and the hills will break
forth into shouts of joy before you,
And all the trees of the field
will clap their hands.

ISAIAH 55:12 NASB

September 12

So let us know, let us press on
   to know the Lord.
His going forth is as certain as the dawn;
And He will come to us like the rain,
Like the spring rain watering the earth.

HOSEA 6:3 NASB

April 21

*A*nd ye shall seek me, and find me, when ye shall search for me with all your heart. And I will be found of you, saith the Lord.

JEREMIAH 29:13–14 KJV

September 11

I will repay you for the years
the locusts have eaten.... And you
will praise the name of the Lord your God,
who has worked wonders for you.

JOEL 2:25-26 NIV

April 22

My Presence will go with you, and I will give you rest.

Exodus 33:14 NIV

September 10

I look behind me and you're there, then
up ahead and you're there, too—your
reassuring presence, coming and going.
This is too much, too wonderful—
I can't take it all in!

PSALM 139:5-6 MSG

April 23

*H*e wants not only us but everyone saved, you know, everyone to get to know the truth we've learned: that there's one God and only one, and one Priest-Mediator between God and us—Jesus, who offered himself in exchange for everyone held captive by sin, to set them all free. Eventually the news is going to get out.

1 TIMOTHY 2:4-6 MSG

September 9

*F*or God so loved the world
that he gave his one and only Son,
that whoever believes in him shall
not perish but have eternal life.

JOHN 3:16 NIV

April 24

*T*hank the Lord for his steadfast love, for his wonderful works to humankind. For he satisfies the thirsty, and the hungry he fills with good things.

PSALM 107:8–9 NRSV

September 8

*B*less the Lord, O you his angels,
you mighty ones who do his bidding....
Bless the Lord, all his works, in
all places of his dominion.
Bless the Lord, O my soul.

PSALM 103:20,22 NRSV

April 25

$\mathcal{L}$isten to me...you whom I have upheld since you were conceived, and have carried since your birth. Even to your old age and gray hairs I am he, I am he who will sustain you. I have made you and I will carry you.

September 7

*A*nd I heard, as it were, the voice of a great multitude and as the sound of many waters and as the sound of mighty peals of thunder, saying, "Hallelujah! For the Lord our God, the Almighty, reigns. Let us rejoice and be glad and give the glory to Him, for the marriage of the Lamb has come and His bride has made herself ready."

REVELATION 19:6–7 NASB

April 26

$\mathcal{W}$e all, like sheep, have gone astray,
each of us has turned to his own way;
and the Lord has laid on him
the iniquity of us all.

ISAIAH 53:6 NIV

September 6

God is our refuge and strength, a very present help in trouble. Therefore will we not fear, though the earth be removed, and though the mountains be carried into the midst of the sea.

PSALM 46:1-3 KJV

April 27

This is my commandment,
That ye love one another,
as I have loved you. Greater
love hath no man than this,
that a man lay down his
life for his friends.

JOHN 15:12-13 KJV

September 5

The eternal God is your refuge,
and underneath are the everlasting arms.

DEUTERONOMY 33:27 NIV

April 28

O Lord, our Lord, how majestic is your name in all the earth! You have set your glory above the heavens.

PSALM 8:1 NIV

September 4

For surely I know the plans I have for you, says the Lord, plans for your welfare and not for harm, to give you a future with hope.

JEREMIAH 29:11 NRSV

April 29

*A*nd the child grew,
and the Lord blessed him.

JUDGES 13:24 KJV

September 3

Your love, O Lord,
reaches to the heavens,
your faithfulness to the skies.

PSALM 36:5 NIV

April 30

He heals the heartbroken and bandages their wounds. He counts the stars and assigns each a name. Our Lord is great, with limitless strength; we'll never comprehend what he knows and does.

PSALM 147:3-5 MSG

September 2

$\mathcal{L}$ove...binds everything together in perfect harmony.

COLOSSIANS 3:14 NRSV

May 1

*F*or everything that was written in the past was written to teach us, so that through endurance and the encouragement of the Scriptures we might have hope.

ROMANS 15:4 NIV

September 1

O the depth of the riches both of the wisdom and knowledge of God! how unsearchable are his judgments, and his ways past finding out! For who hath known the Mind of the Lord? Or who hath been his Counsellor?

ROMANS 11:33–34 KJV

May 2

Be strong and courageous,
do not be afraid or tremble
at them, for the Lord your God
is the one who goes with you.
He will not fail you
or forsake you.

DEUTERONOMY 31:6 NASB

August 31

Trust in the Lord with all your heart
and lean not on your own understanding;
in all your ways acknowledge him,
and he will make your paths straight.

PROVERBS 3:5-6 NIV

May 3

$\mathcal{J}$esus...said to them, "Let the little children come to me; do not stop them; for it is to such as these that the kingdom of God belongs."

MARK 10:14 NRSV

$\mathcal{A}$ugust 30

$\mathcal{T}$he steadfast love of the Lord is from everlasting to everlasting on those who fear him, and his righteousness to children's children.

PSALM 103:17 NRSV

May 4

*H*is huge outstretched arms protect you—
under them you're perfectly safe; his arms
fend off all harm.... No harm will even
graze you. You'll stand untouched,
watch it all from a distance.

PSALM 91:4,8 MSG

August 29

$\mathcal{B}$lessed are they which are persecuted for righteousness sake; for theirs is the kingdom of heaven.

MATTHEW 5:10 KJV

May 5

$\mathcal{B}$lessed are the merciful,
for they will be shown mercy.

MATTHEW 5:7 NIV

August 28

Blessed be the Lord, who has given rest to His people Israel, according to all that He promised; not one word has failed of all His good promise, which He promised through Moses His servant.

1 KINGS 8:56 NASB

May 6

*B*ut we see Jesus, who was made a little lower than the angels for the suffering of death, crowned with glory and honour; that he by the grace of God should taste death for every man.

HEBREWS 2:9 KJV

August 27

*W*hom have I in heaven but you?
And earth has nothing I desire besides you.
My flesh and my heart may fail,
but God is the strength of my heart
and my portion forever.

PSALM 73:25–26 NIV

May 7

But don't, dear friend, resent
God's discipline; don't sulk
under his loving correction.
It's the child he loves that
God corrects; a father's
delight is behind all this.

PROVERBS 3:11–12 MSG

August 26

*B*ut seek ye first the kingdom of God,
and his righteousness; and all these
things shall be added unto you.

MATTHEW 6:33 KJV

May 8

*W*here is the wise man? Where is the scholar? Where is the philosopher of this age? Has not God made foolish the wisdom of the world? For since in the wisdom of God the world through its wisdom did not know him, God was pleased through the foolishness of what was preached to save those who believe.

1 CORINTHIANS 1:20-21 NIV

August 25

The Lord your God is with you, he is mighty to save. He will take great delight in you, he will quiet you with his love, he will rejoice over you with singing.

ZEPHANIAH 3:17 NIV

May 9

$\mathcal{T}$hus saith the Lord, Let not the wise man glory in his wisdom, neither let the mighty man glory in his might, let not the rich man glory in his riches: But let him that glorieth glory in this, that he understandeth and knoweth me, that I am the Lord which exercise lovingkindness, judgment, and righteousness, in the earth: for in these things I delight.

JEREMIAH 9:23-24 KJV

August 24

At that time I will make a treaty.... I will bind you to me forever with chains of righteousness and justice and love and mercy. I will betroth you to me in faithfulness and love, and you will really know me then as you never have before.

HOSEA 2:18-20 TLB

May 10

$\mathcal{L}$ove mixed with faith be yours
from God the Father and from
the Master, Jesus Christ. Pure
grace and nothing but grace
be with all who love our
Master, Jesus Christ.

EPHESIANS 6:23-24 MSG

August 23

$\mathcal{L}$ord, there is no one like you to help the powerless against the mighty. Help us, O Lord our God, for we rely on you, and in your name we have come against this vast army. O Lord, you are our God; do not let man prevail against you.

2 CHRONICLES 14:11 NIV

May 11

$\mathcal{M}$ay they who love you be like the sun when it rises in its strength.

JUDGES 5:31 NIV

August 22

*E*verything in the world is about to be wrapped up, so take nothing for granted. Stay wide-awake in prayer. Most of all, love each other as if your life depended on it. Love makes up for practically anything.

1 PETER 4:7-8 MSG

May 12

He made known to us the mystery of his will according to his good pleasure, which he purposed in Christ, to be put into effect when the times will have reached their fulfillment— to bring all things in heaven and on earth together under one head, even Christ.

EPHESIANS 1:9-10 NIV

August 21

*H*e surrounds me with
lovingkindness and tender mercies.
He fills my life with good things!

PSALM 103:4-5 TLB

May 13

*T*hose who love, I will deliver; I will protect those who know my name. When they call me, I will answer them; I will be with them in trouble, I will rescue them and honor them.

PSALM 91:14–15 NRSV

August 20

*P*leasant words are a honeycomb,
Sweet to the soul and healing to the bones.

PROVERBS 16:24 NASB

May 14

$\mathcal{B}$y this all men will know that you are My disciples, if you have love for one another.

JOHN 13:35 NASB

August 19

$\mathcal{I}$ will praise you, O Lord,
  with all my heart;
I will tell of all your wonders.
I will be glad and rejoice in you;
I will sing praise to your name,
O Most High.

PSALM 9:1-2 NIV

May 15

*Y*et the Lord longs to be gracious to you;
he rises to show you compassion.
For the Lord is a God of justice.
Blessed are all who wait for him!

ISAIAH 30:18 NIV

August 18

$\mathcal{L}$ittle children, let us love, not in word or speech, but in truth and action.

1 JOHN 3:18 NRSV

$\mathcal{M}ay\ 16$

*W*hat a God! His road
stretches straight and smooth.
Every God-direction is road-tested.
Everyone who runs toward him
Makes it.
Is there any god like God?

PSALM 18:30–31 MSG

August 17

$\mathcal{A}$nd we know that all things
work together for good to them
that love God, to them who are
the called according to his purpose.

ROMANS 8:28 KJV

$\mathcal{M}$ay 17

We wait in hope for the Lord;
he is our help and our shield.

PSALM 33:20 NIV

August 16

*B*ut He knows the way I take;
When He has tried me,
I shall come forth as gold.

JOB 23:10 NASB

May 18

$\mathcal{M}$y purpose is that they may be encouraged in heart and united in love, so that they may have the full riches of complete understanding, in order that they may know the mystery of God, namely, Christ, in whom are hidden all the treasures of wisdom and knowledge.

COLOSSIANS 2:2-3 NIV

August 15

For a day in thy courts is better than a thousand. I had rather be a doorkeeper in the house of my God, than to dwell in the tents of wickedness. For the Lord God is a sun and shield: the Lord will give grace and glory: no good thing will he withhold from them that walk uprightly.

PSALM 84:10-11 KJV

May 19

*F*ear not, for I am with you. Do not be dismayed. I am your God. I will strengthen you; I will help you; I will uphold you with my victorious right hand.

ISAIAH 41:10 TLB

August 14

*W*ithout God it is utterly impossible.
But with God everything is possible.

MARK 10:27 TLB

May 20

$\mathcal{B}$lessed is the man that walketh not in the counsel of the ungodly, nor standeth in the way of sinners, nor sitteth in the seat of the scornful. But his delight is in the law of the Lord; and in his law doth he meditate day and night. And he shall be like a tree planted by the rivers of water, that bringeth forth his fruit in his season; his leaf also shall not wither; and whatsoever he doeth shall prosper.

Psalm 1:1-3 KJV

August 13

For Christ's love compels us, because we are convinced that one died for all, and therefore all died. And he died for all, that those who live should no longer live for themselves but for him who died for them and was raised again.... Therefore, if anyone is in Christ, he is a new creation; the old has gone, the new has come!

2 CORINTHIANS 5:14–15,17 NIV

May 21

I am the door: by me if any man
enter in, he shall be saved.

JOHN 10:9 KJV

August 12

Carry each other's burdens, and in this way you will fulfill the law of Christ.

GALATIANS 6:2 NIV

May 22

The sun will no more be your light by day, nor will the brightness of the moon shine on you, for the Lord will be your everlasting light, and your God will be your glory. Your sun will never set again, and your moon will wane no more; the Lord will be your everlasting light, and your days of sorrow will end.

ISAIAH 60:19–20 NIV

August 11

You've always been great toward me—
what love! You snatched me from the
brink of disaster!... You, O God, are
both tender and kind, not easily angered,
immense in love, and you never, never quit.

PSALM 86:13,15 MSG

May 23

How excellent is thy lovingkindness,
O God! therefore the children of men put
their trust under the shadow of thy wings.

PSALM 36:7 KJV

August 10

$\mathcal{S}$ay only what is good and helpful...
and what will give...a blessing.

EPHESIANS 4:29 TLB

λ λ λ λ λ

May 24

$\mathcal{F}$ear not, for I have redeemed you; I have summoned you by name; you are mine. When you pass through the waters, I will be with you; and when you pass through the rivers, they will not sweep over you. When you walk through the fire, you will not be burned; the flames will not set you ablaze.

ISAIAH 43:1-2 NIV

August 9

The righteous cry out, and the Lord hears them; he delivers them from all their troubles. The Lord is close to the brokenhearted and saves those who are crushed in spirit.

PSALM 34:17–18 NIV

May 25

*G*od's love is meteoric,
his loyalty astronomic,
His purpose titanic,
his verdicts oceanic.
Yet in his largeness
nothing gets lost.

PSALM 36:5-6 MSG

August 8

$\mathcal{E}$ver since I heard about your faith in the Lord Jesus and your love for all the saints, I have not stopped giving thanks for you, remembering you in my prayers. I keep asking that the God of our Lord Jesus Christ, the glorious Father, may give you the Spirit of wisdom and revelation, so that you may know him better.

EPHESIANS 1:15-17 NIV

May 26

A glad heart makes a cheerful countenance.... A cheerful heart has a continual feast.

PROVERBS 15:13,15 NRSV

August 7

$\mathscr{T}$he Lord is faithful in all his words,
and gracious in all his deeds.

Psalm 145:13 NRSV

May 27

*T*he Spirit of the Lord God is upon me; because the Lord hath anointed me...to comfort all that mourn...to give unto them beauty for ashes, the oil of joy for mourning, the garment of praise for the spirit of heaviness; that they might be called trees of righteousness, the planting of the Lord, that he might be glorified.

ISAIAH 61:1,3 KJV

August 6

Surely he hath borne our griefs, and carried our sorrows: yet we did esteem him stricken, smitten of God, and afflicted. But he was wounded for our transgressions, he was bruised for our iniquities: the chastisement of our peace was upon him; and with his stripes we are healed.

ISAIAH 53:4–5 KJV

May 28

The angel of the Lord encamps around those who fear him, and he delivers them.

PSALM 34:7 NIV

August 5

*G*race, mercy and peace from God the Father and from Jesus Christ, the Father's Son, will be with us in truth and love.

2 JOHN 1:3 NIV

May 29

I pray that you, being rooted and established in love, may have power, together with all the saints, to grasp how wide and long and high and deep is the love of Christ, and to know this love that surpasses knowledge—that you may be filled to the measure of all the fullness of God.

EPHESIANS 3:17–19 NIV

August 4

*I*n the beginning was the Word, and the Word was with God, and the Word was God. The same was in the beginning with God. All things were made by him; and without him was not any thing made that was made. In him was life; and the life was the light of men.

JOHN 1:1-4 KJV

May 30

*A*s for me and my house, we will serve the Lord.

JOSHUA 24:15 KJV

August 3

Since God assured us,
"I'll never let you down,
never walk off and leave you,"
we can boldly quote,
"God is there, ready to help;
I'm fearless no matter what.
Who or what can get to me?"

HEBREWS 13:5-6 MSG

May 31

*P*raise be to the name of God for ever and ever; wisdom and power are his. He changes times and seasons; he sets up kings and deposes them. He gives wisdom to the wise and knowledge to the discerning. He reveals deep and hidden things; he knows what lies in darkness, and light dwells with him.

DANIEL 2:20-22 NIV

August 2

The Lord gives strength to his people;
the Lord blesses his people with peace.

PSALM 29:11 NIV

June 1

*F*or he will command his angels concerning you to guard you in all your ways; they will lift you up in their hands, so that you will not strike your foot against a stone.

PSALM 91:11-12 NIV

August 1

Go ye therefore, and teach all nations...
teaching them to observe all things
whatsoever I have commanded you:
and, lo, I am with you always, even
unto the end of the world.

MATTHEW 28:19-20 KJV

June 2

*H*e will yet fill your mouth with laughter
and your lips with shouts of joy.

JOB 8:21 NIV

July 31

*B*e imitators of God,
as beloved children,
and live in love,
as Christ loved us.

EPHESIANS 5:1-2 NRSV

June 3

I will lift up mine eyes unto the hills,
from whence cometh my help.
My help cometh from the Lord,
which made heaven and earth.

PSALM 121:1–2 KJV

July 30

The Lord will guide you always; he will
satisfy your needs in a sun-scorched land....
You will be like a well-watered garden,
like a spring whose waters never fail.

ISAIAH 58:11 NIV

June 4

*A*nd God raised us up with Christ and seated us with him in the heavenly realms in Christ Jesus, in order that in the coming ages he might show the incomparable riches of his grace, expressed in his kindness to us in Christ Jesus.

EPHESIANS 2:6-7 NIV

July 29

$\mathcal{Y}$our goodness and unfailing kindness shall be with me all of my life, and afterwards I will live with you forever in your home.

PSALM 23:6 TLB

$\mathcal{June}$ 5

$\mathcal{T}$he steadfast love of the Lord never ceases, his mercies never come to an end; they are new every morning; great is your faithfulness.

LAMENTATIONS 3:22-23 NRSV

July 28

*Y*ou have made known
to me the paths of life;
you will fill me with joy
in your presence.

ACTS 2:28 NIV

June 6

You have not come to a mountain that can be touched.... But you have come to Mount Zion, to the heavenly Jerusalem, the city of the living God. You have come to thousands upon thousands of angels in joyful assembly, to the church of the firstborn, whose names are written in heaven. You have come to God, the judge of all men...to Jesus the mediator of a new covenant.

HEBREWS 12:18,22-24 NIV

July 27

*Hope deferred makes the heart sick,
but a longing fulfilled is a tree of life.*

PROVERBS 13:12 NIV

June 7

*Y*ou guide me with your counsel,
and afterward you will receive
me with honor.

PSALM 73:24 NRSV

July 26

$\mathcal{B}$e not forgetful to entertain strangers:
for thereby some have entertained
angels unawares.

HEBREWS 13:2 KJV

June 8

For he is the living God
and he endures forever;
his kingdom will not be destroyed,
his dominion will never end.
He rescues and he saves;
he performs signs and wonders
in the heavens and on the earth.

DANIEL 6:26–27 NIV

July 25

I have thoroughly tested your promises
and that is why I love them so much.

PSALM 119:140 TLB

June 9

*Y*es, because God's your refuge,
the High God your very own home,
Evil can't get close to you, harm
can't get through the door.
He ordered his angels to
guard you wherever you go.

PSALM 91:9-11 MSG

July 24

I've learned by now to be quite content whatever my circumstances. I'm just as happy with little as with much, with much as with little. I've found the recipe for being happy whether full or hungry, hands full or hands empty. Whatever I have, wherever I am, I can make it through anything in the One who makes me who I am.

PHILIPPIANS 4:11-13 MSG

June 10

"*Peace* I leave with you,
my peace I give unto you:
not as the world giveth,
give I unto you. Let not
your heart be troubled,
neither let it be afraid."

JOHN 14:27 KJV

July 23

$\mathcal{Y}$es, Lord, walking in the way of your laws, we wait for you; your name and renown are the desire of our hearts. My soul yearns for you in the night; in the morning my spirit longs for you.

ISAIAH 26:8 NIV

$\mathcal{June}$ 11

$\mathcal{N}$ow that we know what we have—Jesus, this great High Priest with ready access to God—let's not let it slip through our fingers. We don't have a priest who is out of touch with our reality. He's been through weakness and testing, experienced it all—all but the sin. So let's walk right up to him and get what he is so ready to give. Take the mercy, accept the help.

HEBREWS 4:14-16 MSG

July 22

Bring ye all the tithes into the storehouse...
and prove me now herewith, saith the
Lord of hosts, if I will not open you the
windows of heaven, and pour you out
a blessing, that there shall not be
room enough to receive it.

MALACHI 3:10 KJV

June 12

Give generously, for your
gifts will return to you later.

ECCLESIASTES 11:1 TLB

July 21

F or in Him all the fullness of Deity dwells in bodily form, and in Him you have been made complete, and He is the head over all rule and authority.

COLOSSIANS 2:9-10 NASB

June 13

*H*ave not I commanded you?
Be strong and courageous!
Do not tremble or be dismayed,
for the Lord your God is with
you wherever you go.

JOSHUA 1:9 NASB

July 20

$\mathcal{T}$hese commandments that I give you today are to be upon your hearts. Impress them on your children. Talk about them when you sit at home and when you walk along the road, when you lie down and when you get up.

DEUTERONOMY 6:6-7 NIV

June 14

When he saw the crowds, he had compassion on them, because they were harassed and helpless, like sheep without a shepherd. Then he said to his disciples, "The harvest is plentiful but the workers are few. Ask the Lord of the harvest, therefore, to send out workers into his harvest field."

MATTHEW 9:36-38 NIV

July 19

$\mathcal{W}$ith my whole heart have I sought thee: O let me not wander from thy commandments. Thy word have I hid in mine heart, that I might not sin against thee.... I will delight myself in thy statutes: I will not forget thy word.

PSALM 119:10-11,16 KJV

$\mathcal{J}$une 15

*P*rove me, O Lord, and try me; test my heart and mind. For your steadfast love is before my eyes, and I walk in faithfulness to you.

PSALM 26:2-3 NRSV

July 18

$\mathcal{C}$ome to me, all you that are weary and are carrying heavy burdens, and I will give you rest. Take my yoke upon you, and learn from me; for I am gentle and humble in heart, and you will find rest for your souls. For my yoke is easy, and my burden is light.

MATTHEW 11:28–30 NRSV

$\mathcal{June}$ 16

*A*nd when we obey him, every path
he guides us on is fragrant with his
lovingkindness and his truth.

PSALM 25:10 TLB

July 17

$\mathcal{W}$e can rejoice, too, when we run into problems and trials, for we know that they are good for us—they help us learn to be patient. And patience develops strength of character in us and helps us trust God more each time we use it until finally our hope and faith are strong and steady.

ROMANS 5:3-4 TLB

June 17

$\mathcal{B}$ut the path of the righteous
is like the light of dawn,
That shines brighter and brighter
until the full day.

PROVERBS 4:18 NASB

July 16

But for you who revere my name,
the sun of righteousness will rise
with healing in its wings.

MALACHI 4:2 NIV

June 18

Confess your faults one to another,
and pray one for another,
that ye may be healed.
The effectual fervent prayer
of a righteous man availeth much.

JAMES 5:16 KJV

July 15

$\mathcal{J}$esus said, "I am the Bread of Life. The person who aligns with me hungers no more and thirsts no more, ever.... Whoever believes in me has real life, eternal life."

JOHN 6:35,47 MSG

$\mathcal{J}$une 19

I am the Lord, and there is no other; apart from me there is no God. I will strengthen you, though you have not acknowledged me, so that from the rising of the sun to the place of its setting men may know there is none besides me.

ISAIAH 45:5-6 NIV

July 14

$\mathcal{W}$hen I consider thy heavens, the work of thy fingers, the moon and the stars, which thou hast ordained; What is man, that thou art mindful of him? and the son of man, that thou visitest him? For thou hast made him a little lower than the angels, and hast crowned him with glory and honour.

PSALM 8:3–5 KJV

June 20

$\mathcal{B}$e devoted to one another in brotherly love.
Honor one another above yourselves.

Romans 12:10 NIV

July 13

$\mathcal{N}$ow to him who by the power at work within us is able to accomplish abundantly far more than all we can ask or imagine, to him be glory in the church and in Christ Jesus to all generations, forever and ever. Amen.

EPHESIANS 3:20-21 NRSV

$\mathcal{June}$ 21

$\mathcal{P}$repare your minds for action;
be self-controlled; set your hope fully
on the grace to be given you when
Jesus Christ is revealed.

1 PETER 1:13 NIV

July 12

I lavish my love upon thousands of those who love me and obey my commandments.

EXODUS 20:6 TLB

June 22

So spacious is [Christ], so roomy, that everything of God finds its proper place in him without crowding. Not only that, but all the broken and dislocated pieces of the universe—people and things, animals and atoms—get properly fixed and fit together in vibrant harmonies.

COLOSSIANS 1:19-20 MSG

July 11

I thank my God every time
I remember you. In all
my prayers for all of you,
I always pray with joy.

PHILIPPIANS 1:3-4 NIV

June 23

I am he that liveth, and was dead;
and, behold, I am alive for evermore.

REVELATION 1:18 KJV

July 10

$\mathcal{M}$y God is changeless in his love
for me, and he will come and help me.

PSALM 59:10 TLB

June 24

*L*oose the chains of injustice and untie the cords of the yoke.... Then your light will break forth like the dawn, and your healing will quickly appear; then your righteousness will go before you, and the glory of the Lord will be your rear guard.

ISAIAH 58:6,8 NIV

July 9

Holy, holy, holy, is the Lord of hosts:
the whole earth is full of his glory.

ISAIAH 6:3 KJV

June 25

*R*eliable friends who do what they say
are like cool drinks in sweltering heat—
refreshing!

PROVERBS 25:13 MSG

July 8

$\mathcal{F}$or, lo, the winter is past, the rain is over and gone; the flowers appear on the earth; the time of the singing of birds is come.

SONG OF SOLOMON 2:11–12 KJV

June 26

*T*his is the day which the Lord hath made;
we will rejoice and be glad in it.

PSALM 118:24 KJV

July 7

*O*h, give thanks to the Lord,
for he is good; his love and his
kindness go on forever.

1 CHRONICLES 16:34 TLB

June 27

*B*ecause of his great love for us, God, who is rich in mercy, made us alive with Christ even when we were dead in transgressions.... For it is by grace you have been saved, through faith—and this not from yourselves, it is the gift of God—not by works, so that no one can boast.

EPHESIANS 2:4,8-9 NIV

July 6

$\mathcal{T}$he deeper your love, the higher it goes;
every cloud is a flag to your faithfulness.
Soar high in the skies, O God!
Cover the whole earth with your glory!

PSALM 57:10-11 MSG

$\mathcal{J}$une 28

Is anyone thirsty? Come!
All who will, come and drink,
Drink freely of the Water of Life!

REVELATION 22:17 MSG

July 5

*A*s long as I am in the world,
I am the light of the world.

JOHN 9:5 KJV

June 29

$\mathcal{B}$lessed is the nation whose God is the Lord.

PSALM 33:12 NIV

July 4

He himself bore our sins in his body
on the cross, so that, free from sins,
we might live for righteousness;
by his wounds you have been healed.

1 PETER 2:24 NRSV

June 30

$\mathcal{T}$hough the fig tree does not bud
and there are no grapes on the vines,
though the olive crop fails and
the fields produce no food...
yet I will rejoice in the Lord,
I will be joyful in God my Savior.

HABAKKUK 3:17-18 NIV

July 3

$\mathcal{A}$ friend loves at all times.

PROVERBS 17:17 NIV

July 1

*E*very good gift and every perfect gift is from above, and cometh down from the Father of lights, with whom is no variableness, neither shadow of turning.

JAMES 1:17 KJV

July 2